T0275725

Next Generation Red Teaming

Next Generation Red Teaming

Henry Dalziel

Contributing editor
Robert Wood

AMSTERDAM • BOSTON • HEIDELBERG • LONDON
NEW YORK • OXFORD • PARIS • SAN DIEGO
SAN FRANCISCO • SINGAPORE • SYDNEY • TOKYO

SYNGRESS.

ELSEVIER   Syngress is an imprint of Elsevier

Syngress is an imprint of Elsevier
225 Wyman Street, Waltham, MA 02451, USA

ISBN: 978-0-12-804171-0

British Library Cataloguing-in-Publication Data
A catalogue record for this book is available from the British Library

Library of Congress Cataloging-in-Publication Data
A catalog record for this book is available from the Library of Congress

For Information on all Syngress publications
visit our website at http://store.elsevier.com/

  Working together
to grow libraries in
developing countries

www.elsevier.com • www.bookaid.org

CONTENTS

AUTHOR BIOGRAPHY

Henry Dalziel is a serial education entrepreneur, founder of Concise Ac Ltd, online cybersecurity blogger and e-book author. He writes for the Concise-Courses.com blog and has developed numerous cybersecurity continuing education courses and books. Concise Ac Ltd develops and distributes continuing education content [books and courses] for cybersecurity professionals seeking skill enhancement and career advancement. The company was recently accepted onto the UK Trade & Investment's (UKTI) Global Entrepreneur Programme (GEP).

CONTRIBUTING EDITOR BIOGRAPHY

Robert Wood is a Technical Manager at Cigital and leads the development and execution of the red team assessment practice for the firm. Robert has worked with a number of clients spanning from Fortune 100 financial institutions to gaming companies providing services at every stage in the SDLC. Prior to Cigital, Robert worked for Secure Network Technologies where he developed the mobile forensic investigation practice and focused his penetration testing efforts on red teaming and network security assessments.

CHAPTER 1

Introduction

In this book, we explain what "red teaming" is, and how it differs from the traditional penetration test and associated methodologies. We start by reviewing the standard industry approach to red teaming and share several ways that this approach could be improved. We then describe how to build a successful red team, regardless of whether you're outsourcing your requirements or building a red team internally. We discuss how to quantify the various adversaries that your organization will go up against, including differences between threat actors such as script kiddies versus a nation state. Each adversary has different capabilities and motivations and therefore must be modeled accordingly to drive effective defense.

The latter part of this book covers one of the biggest differences or deviations from what we believe quantifies a successful red team: the lack of software-based analysis in the process. We'll talk about how to incorporate software-based testing and software-based analysis and then cover composite attack development. We'll explain what composite attacks are in the context of a red team assessment and then how to bridge the gap between red team testing and all of the defensive capabilities that go into a security program, such as incidence response, attack monitoring, and threat intelligence.

And finally, we get into building an effective red team program (versus just doing a one-off assessment). Ultimately the "program approach" that this book proposes is more sustainable and holds more value across a large organization and will ultimately help you (and your organization) get the most out of the red team process.

What Is Red Teaming?

- Goal-based adversarial testing process

- Organizational assessment versus testing a specific target in a vacuum

- Measures how an organization will actually respond to an attack

- Incorporates many elements of an organization's overall security posture

Red teaming as a whole is a goal-based adversarial testing process. What we mean by this is, as opposed to a traditional penetration test or vulnerability scan, where you have a target, let's say, a web application, server, or group of people who you're going to conduct social engineering tests on, the traditional penetration test will take that target, and try to find as many vulnerabilities associated with it as possible. So, for example, if you're looking at a web server and SSL configurations, you may have missing patches or be accepting weak SSL ciphers; you may have an insecure operating system or web server software version; you may have a number of other configuration issues on that operating system or server. Beyond that server, within the context of an enterprise network for instance, you really don't know how those individual issues affect the greater system level perspective, i.e., the organization as a whole.

Conversely, a red team approach takes a holistic organization-wide approach. So as a red teamer, everything that we do while testing an organization is going to be goal-based. We define a goal at the start of the assessment, such as compromise customer data, cryptographic keys, or figuring out ways to get access to an internal network so that we can establish a foothold in a customer's network, sit there, and wait for sensitive information so that we can capture it and move on, or siphon it off to a command and control server. Whatever our goal is at the outset of the assessment, everything that we do should move us one step closer to achieving that goal, much in the same way that an attacker operates. It's important to remember that attackers don't want to find a bunch of vulnerabilities; they want to find the right vulnerabilities that let them accomplish their goals!

So, a red team assessment is ultimately a simulated attack effort that targets a defined set of goals. You have good guys playing the attackers, or modeling the attackers. They use the same tools, techniques, and methods that a real hacker would. As part of this process, you can have a red team versus a blue team scenario, where you get to see how the functional components of the organization respond to different types of attacks. We want to find out whether the organization can prevent those attacks from succeeding in the first place, detecting those attacks if they do succeed, and respond to them, returning the organization into a state of normalcy and homeostasis.

Red teams incorporate different elements across an organization's security posture, depending on whether it's a government agency or a large financial institution. We incorporate network systems, and various types of software and mobile apps. We incorporate business processes such as how new vendors get incorporated into workflows, or how new employees get onboarded. There are a lot of different elements that can affect an organization's security posture. In a red team assessment, we're going to be considering all of those as we develop composite attacks.

CHAPTER 2

The Typical Approach

The Typical Approach

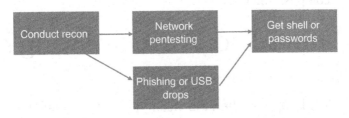

So let's begin by reviewing the typical approach. If you go online and search for "how do I red team," the search results typically start with open-source intelligence (OSINT) reconnaissance ("Reconnaissance"). Reconnaissance covers activities such as identifying the attack surface, looking at the various IP address blocks that you are coming up against; trying to identify related web sites; their official mobile apps; exposed Application Program Interface (APIs) that the mobile apps are interacting with; employee names, etc. Simply put, reconnaissance can be looked at as the glue that holds the red team together.

The standard approach will then proceed to network penetration testing ("pentesting"). Pentesting as a whole is a mature process when compared to software-based testing (which is rapidly catching up) and focuses mostly on getting shells and compromising systems.

Often, you'll also see red teams incorporate various types of phishing and/or USB drop attacks. What we mean by that is when you launch any of these attacks, the goal is to get either a user's password or have them run some kind of executable code that gives the attacker access to their system on a remote basis. From there we'll get a shell or passwords, and often times, that's where you'll see the typical approach end.

From a real-world attacker's perspective, they don't necessarily care about compromising one user's system. If we look at the case of the recent Target incident,[1] it started with a phishing attack on an Heating, Ventilating and Air Conditioning (HVAC) vendor that worked for them. If the attack had stopped there, it would never have made headlines. What made this attack work was the fact that they took that access, pivoted, got somewhere else, and just kept traversing through Target's network until they were able to compromise customer data. The takeaway is that you can't just stop after getting passwords, getting shell, running executable code, etc. You need to go further; you need to accomplish the goal.

Where Did We Go Wrong?

- What about the software?

- What happens when the victim quits or changes their password?

- What "asset" did we really compromise?

- What did we learn about the overall security posture?

- What did we learn about the incident response procedures?

The typical red team approach does not include software security testing. It doesn't consider any of the organization's web sites or mobile apps for example. Simply put, we do not consider anything related to software.

Let's also consider what might happen when "the employee" who fell for your phishing attack quits, or changes their password (because they got a new dog!). In that case the value of your single compromise degrades.

The traditional approach should also factor in how to articulate return-on-investment to senior management. In the scenario outlined above, we can't really say that we did anything—we got a password, we got a shell. We got something, whatever that thing was, but if there

---

[1]Epic Target hack reportedly began with malware-based phishing e-mail. http://arstechnica.com/security/2014/02/epic-target-hack-reportedly-began-with-malware-based-phishing-e-mail/.

was nothing sensitive on that user's system, if they didn't have the crown jewels to their organization on their desktop, then the impact of the attack becomes somewhat nullified.

Furthermore, the traditional approach doesn't really teach us about the organization's overall security posture. We have not learned how they respond to attacks or how they detect attacks. We don't know if there are any downstream controls that would have prevented a successful pivot attack to something sensitive. Are there other vectors across the organization that may be a better focus for certain types of attackers? We don't really have this level of insight with the traditional approach.

CHAPTER 3

Red Team Assessment

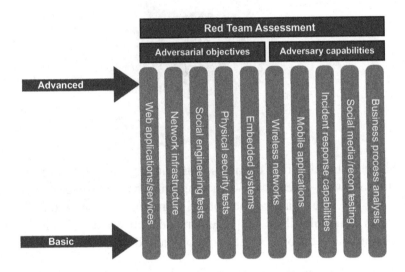

This diagram highlights one of the largest differences between penetration testing and red teaming. If we look at each of the vertical blocks as an individual target or potential target, you'll see that we have web applications/web services, we've got various types of network infrastructure. We've got wireless testing, mobile applications, embedded systems, and so on. Really, in any kind of penetration test, we can have a very advanced assessment of the target (i.e., a deep dive manual test), and on the lower end, we can conduct a basic test. The basic assessment would be the quick automated scan such as your Nessus and Burp Suite scans. Basic assessments catch a lot of the "low hanging fruit," but they really don't test any design-focused or more embedded, rooted issues in the system we're looking at.

A red team assessment takes the adversary mind-set and capabilities along with the adversarial objectives that you are working with, and it sits like an umbrella over this entire suite of different assessment techniques and targets that you can employ.

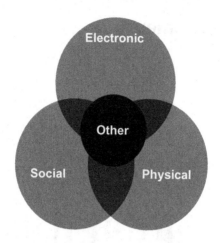

Some of the different elements that might go into this can be seen in the following three-part Venn diagram: the electronic, the social, and physical. We've added the "other" component to show the various elements that pull all of this together and that doesn't fit nicely into the traditional electronic, social, and physical domains.

Electronic	Social	Physical	Other activities
Software	Phishing	Access control technologies	OSINT recon
Network	Phone-based	Physical facility security	Business process analysis
Wireless technologies	IM/chat	Access badge processes	Attack intelligence/ modeling
Platforms and infrastracture	Social media mining	Employee and vendor onboarding	Incident response evaluation
Mobile technologies			Risk management
Embedded technologies			Role-based social engineering

Electronic is self-explanatory—it's anything digital, anything technical, anything that we can go out and hack.

The social domain means anything that involves people. In other words, if you are launching phishing attacks, calling your target on the phone, or cataloging information via your targets Facebook, Twitter or Instagram account.

The physical domain focuses on how employees are accessing the office in the mornings, after their breaks and of course when they leave at the end of the day. Do they do everything by lock and key and then just be polite, and hold the door for people, or do they use access cards? If they use access cards, what kinds of access cards do they use? Can they be easily cloned and replayed? Are they easily cloned using readily available code and/or off the shelf tools? How do they issue new access badges? In other words, if I'm a new employee and I lose my access badge, or leave it at home, can I get a replacement badge for the day? Do I just show my business card and get a temporary badge, or is it more involved? Understanding these processes is exactly what an attacker is going to do, and they're going to look for places where they may be able to inject themselves and potentially spoof certain things or bypass certain controls if there's a weaker area and get around obstacles to get an access badge or get access to a building.

"Other activities" include activities such as OSINT reconnaissance, the biggest foundation to a red team assessment. In order to intelligently attack an organization you need to understand that organization. You cannot treat a large government agency the same way that you would treat a small insurance company or law firm. These organizations have different attack surfaces; they function in different ways. They have different technology stacks that they use for different purposes. You need to intimately understand your targets to attack them in a way that a red team is going to be impacted.

Business process analysis looks at, for example, how the organization manages vendor supply chains. How they order new systems or new computer components. How they onboard new employees or vendors. How they handle shipping and delivery to their offices. All of these elements are potential areas of organizational vulnerability that can be attacked by the right adversary.

Attack intelligence and attack modeling is where we get into the composite attack creation that we'll talk about a little bit later.

Incident response evaluation is where you start to understand and take note of what you are doing, so that way you can tie that back into the incident response capability then we'll talk about later with the bridge of the attack and defense components.

Risk management is where an attacker takes advantage of how an organization performs risk management. For example, a high-risk component gets a lot of attention and a low-risk component does not with regard to security. However, if there is a connection between those high- and low-risk components that could be exploitable, then an attacker can go after that low-risk component and get access to the high-risk one in a nontraditional manner. We'll discuss this in more detail later on too.

Role-based social engineering is another "next generation activity" that we'd like to encourage. Role-based social engineering differs from point in time social engineering, or targeted social engineering where, for example, we would be social engineering Mary from HR or Joe from Finance, i.e., a very specific individual in a very specific role.

Role-based social engineering is where we take a role such as a customer service representative. And that customer service representative, for example, has the authority to help customers with password resets. Any given person that fits into that role is going to follow a certain script and workflow. If there are weaknesses in the way that the system is designed, let's say the process has been designed in such a way that a password reset requires the customer share his/her social security number. Let's say the customer representative can view social security numbers directly on the screen, which leaves them susceptible to being stolen, or the social security numbers are being stored in plain text, as opposed to the system being set up where the customer representative needs to enter them in character by character when performing a quick validation. Or perhaps the customer service representative can see all of the answers to the security questions that are there, so an attacker could say: "well, what street did I grow up on? You know it might have been Main Street, it might have been Winks Avenue, I'm not sure what I provided for that answer." The customer service representative could then be encouraged to say; "you know we actually have

Main Street here. Okay, great." In other words, a savvy hacker can smooth talk the representative into getting around certain steps in the process. Basically the goal with role-based social engineering is to find issues in a workflow that allows you to extrapolate those issues to any person who would fit into that particular role. Anybody could be susceptible to social engineering and fixing the individual is not necessarily the problem. We want to design secure systems and workflows to protect people from themselves, from being susceptible to such attacks.

CHAPTER 4

Elements for Success

Elements for Success

- Bring business context into the picture

- Assets make headlines, not simple vulnerabilities

- A good red team is made up of various backgrounds, skill sets, and mind-sets

- Diversity breeds excellence in these assessments to avoid group think conditions

- Assessment is iterative not linear, you can always learn, test, learn more, and then revisit the drawing board

Moving into the elements for success, if you're building up one of these types of engagements internally or you're outsourcing it, there's a few different things that you want to make sure you look for in either case. The first one is to make sure that you always bring business context into the picture. We always want to make sure that you understand what the business does, how it does it, their business goals, risks to those goals, etc. We want to make sure that we understand those assets that the business controls, whether it's customer financial data, PII, PHI for a health care organization, intellectual property for defense firms, or highly sensitive classified information for government agencies. Whatever the case may be, any organization has assets, and it's the assets that make headlines when they're compromised, not the very simple cross-site scripting or SQL injection, or that ABC gets their system rooted and somebody has a shell on it.

Ultimately moving past that, a good red team is going to be made up of a variety of different backgrounds and skill sets. One of the reasons that we want to do that when we're building our team is to avoid having five people with the exact same background, the exact same skill set and mind-set. We don't only want one way of thinking when we look at the common denominators among all of them. All of them are going to be thinking and trying and working out the same kinds of attacks as opposed to if we have five different professionals with different approaches to things, different ways of thinking, different specialties then they're all going to be looking at the system from a different perspective and we're going to get a lot more coverage, a lot more value out of all that testing.

Building off of that "diversity," in this case, is really what breeds excellence. When you avoid the groupthink, i.e., where everyone is thinking in exactly the same manner, and you can sit down and sit at a whiteboard or sit in a conference room and really just talk through scenarios and everyone is bouncing ideas off one another: "would this particular scenario work? No, because from my domain I think XYZ controls would be in place. Okay, how about this"? You can really work through some very interesting composite attacks when you have a diverse team.

The other factor to note is that red team assessments in particular are a very iterative process. The longer that you can structure them out/drag them out, and drag has kind of a negative connotation in this case, but it's actually very positive, the better off you are going to be in the long term in getting results out of the red team assessment.

Basically the attackers, the advanced persistent threat, and the targeted threat are going to take as much time as they need; time is not as much of an element to these hackers as it is for a traditional vulnerability scanner or pentest where you take, let's say, a two-week period and you block it out and you say we're going to take and test your target, or rather, test our target based on a snapshot of what it was at the start of that two weeks and we're going to test it through to the end of two weeks. At the end of that time period, that's the end of the test; we're going to write up a bunch of vulnerabilities for you and we're going to go on to the next thing.

In a red team assessment, you want your red team to go out, learn, try things, fail a little bit and face some resistance, have a little bit of success, go back to the drawing board, think of new things, go out, learn more, test more, and just keep pushing toward those composite attacks that actually work and get them access to the adversarial goals that they're targeting. Ultimately it's when you can iterate through various test cases that you truly understand the different complexities that go into a modern enterprise, or a very complex organization.

COMPOSITE ATTACK CASE STUDY

We'd like to share a composite attack that we worked on a couple of years ago with a defense agency and what we did to get access to their intellectual property. To set the scene, our goal was to get access to this defense firm's intellectual property. We were told that their intellectual property was stored in an internal only application with a back-end database. Most of their employees had access to it, all of their engineering teams, and some management. You had to be on the internal network and they were convinced that their internal network was the "end-all, be-all." We were emulating a very targeted criminal organization, or potential terrorist group given the nature of their business, and the kind of government agencies they were working with and the data they were collecting.

So we did our due diligence. We started by learning about all of their external assets, external network systems, their VPN, end points, etc. We didn't really get anywhere doing any of that testing. We did some basic phishing, but it turned out everyone was sandboxed away from any real important corporate assets.

What we did, however, was show up and perform a variety of onsite physical attacks at their headquarters. One of the most entertaining ones, and what we'll talk about here, is we got ourselves some FedEx uniforms and with those FedEx uniforms we got a very big pelican supply case, and we took it to a machine shop and had it modified in a few select ways. We put a little periscope on the top part of the case. We made some false latches for the front and we put real latches on the inside sides of the case. We made a few other modifications—we loaded it with several Pwn Plugs and other interesting testing tools that would allow somebody on the inside to take advantage of that access.

We then took the smallest member of our team and stuffed him inside the box! He was also dressed as an employee. We had employee uniforms made up and we took him and all the tools and put him inside. Then we got a couple of handcarts and wheeled him into the building and delivered him as FedEx Custom Critical employees. While we were there, they accepted the package, they wheeled him up, and they had a supply closet up near their executive offices and conference rooms. He was able to wait until after business hours and once he was out of the box, he was able to install Pwn Plugs in all of the executive offices and several conference rooms. From there we had access to the internal network. So we did more scanning with that internal access. Found a few open network shares, hacked a few systems, caught some traffic going around the wire. Then we came across the internal application that apparently housed all the intellectual property and what our real target was. Upon going to it we realized that it was a homegrown application and often times internal homegrown applications have a lot of issues because regardless of what they're storing, they are internal and people are writing them themselves and they're often times just whipped up quickly to solve a very critical business need. They are not given a lot of thought with regard to the risk management process. In this particular case we found a very basic SQL injection issue on the login page of the application that allowed us to get access to pretty much any account that we wanted. This gave us the ability to enumerate user names based on, of course, our knowledge of people's e-mails, so we already knew a lot of them, but they had differences in error messages so we could enumerate other user names we didn't necessarily know about and then use a very basic SQL injection payload in the password field and get access to that user's account by authenticating as them. Once we were in, of course, for any valid account that had the correct access control policies enabled, we were able to access all of the intellectual property and save it to our systems.

Business Goals and Risks

- Work with your client or executive sponsors to identify primary goals for the organization and what risks keep them up at night

- A business risk is defined as something that negatively impacts a business goal in this context

- Issues that are identified and all analysis should be tied back to how they impact business goals

- FYI...this is a great thing to take care of during scoping

Ultimately the business goals and risks are one of the biggest concerns that any red team should keep in mind when working through and writing up any kind of results. The reason we say this is that for any red team to be successful it's going to need some level of executive sponsorship or an executive team to sponsor the effort. It's only when you get that level of support that you can inflict real change, where the vulnerabilities that you find will be presented and escalated to the appropriate decision makers. When you can map technical vulnerabilities or composite attacks that you developed back to a string of business goals that are directly impacted by your attack, you can accurately answer the question "who cares." Here's why you should care: because it affects customer data. Here's how we went from zero access to getting access to information, you know, nine out of ten employees were found putting stuff out on social media that allowed us to do this and it's all freely accessible. When you can answer those questions to executive sponsors, you'll be able to inflict real change at the organization, which is hopefully the real goal of any red team, whether you're standing it up internally or outsourcing the effort. Handling these things, so identifying what the business goals are, what the risks to those goals are is a great item to take care of during the scoping process. It complicates the process a lot when you are halfway through and somebody throws a wrench in your plans and says "oh, we're actually concerned about this over here that you haven't spent any time looking at just yet." You can of course adapt, but it just makes things a little bit more difficult.

CHAPTER 5

Who Are We Up Against

Who Are We Up Against?

- Red teaming is a useful process in many situations, not just hacker "stuff"
- An adversary can emerge and cause harm to an organization in many different ways
  - Terrorist groups or nation states
  - Criminal organizations or coordinated hacking groups
  - Individual hackers, reverse engineers, game cheats
  - Competitor targeting intellectual property
  - Many more, use your imagination...

"Who Are We Up Against," is really about understanding who the adversary is that you want your red team to model. Of course each of these adversaries are very different and they all have their own capabilities, their own motivations, and they can all cause harm to our organization in a lot of different ways. If you end up getting targeted by a terrorist group or a nation state, they may have very politically motivated goals and they may be going after physical infrastructure, they may be going after denial of service type attacks and things like that, versus a criminal organization or a hacktivist group, for instance, that might be going after something more financially motivated. Where they are going to be maintaining stealth above all things and just trying to steal data that they can then turn around and sell. Understanding all of these different things are important in how you want your red team to act, because it's not just random hacking, it's all about targeting and modeling a certain adversary because the kinds of things that you are going to look for, the kinds of access that you start with, the kinds of knowledge that you have. Everything has to be central around what adversary you're modeling.

Understand Your Adversary

- All adversaries are unique

  - Motivated by different things (i.e., terrorist cell vs hacktivist group)

  - Very wide range of capabilities

- Understanding what you're up against (or supposed to model) is the first big step

Of course, all adversaries are unique to some degree; they are all motivated by different things. We mentioned the terrorist cell versus the hacktivist group, or the criminal organization versus the insider threat. Let's say that across a terrorist group, criminal organization, and insider threat, you may have political goals, financial goals, and revenge-based goals, respectively, for those three different threat actors. These are three very different goals and each of these motivations are going to determine and influence the kinds of attacks that these adversaries are likely to attempt against your organization, of course also subject to the adversaries' capabilities. This is really the first big step, so this is another thing that you want to understand before you actually get started with a lot of the testing.

Quantify

- We can systematically break down our adversaries capabilities to build a better model:

  - Financial resources

  - Primary motivation(s)

  - Technical, SE, and physical security skills

  - Intensity to achieve their objective

  - Time and personnel they can dedicate

  - Access to kinetic or target resources (i.e., domain services, trust from a vendor relationship, weapons, explosives, etc.)

Quantifying the adversary is the process where we really go through and systematically break down everything about, or as much about our adversaries as we possibly can to build a better model for our red team to go through and work with. As an example, if you as an adversary have a lot of financial resources you may be able to outsource some of the skills that you may be lacking or purchase certain equipment that you don't have. Versus if you don't have a lot of financial resources and you're just functioning on your own, such as the individual hacker threat actor. Let's say you're in the entertainment space and these potential threat actors are going to be working and relying on nothing but their technical skills and maybe the community around whatever they are doing to support them. It's all going to be knowledge-based; their biggest capability is their knowledge in this particular instance.

Sample Adversary

Adversary	Threat profile										
	Commitment				Resources				Skills and capabilities		
	Intensity	Stealth	Time	Primary motivation	Personnel	Kinetic	Access	Technical	Physical security	Social engineering	Financial resources
Skilled remote attacker	H	H →	Weeks	Financial	2 - 9	N/A	L	H	N/A	H	M

A truly dedicated attacker will spend as much time as they need to achieve their goal

This is a sample table of a threat actor or a threat profile that we built out. You'll see a number of different categories, and actually the ones that we use are a little bit longer. Basically we try to assign values to each of these different capability areas so we can quantify in a standard way things like their physical security prowess, their technical prowess, and the level of access that they start with.

One example of how different variables can influence one another is the intensity in which an attacker is dedicated to accomplishing some goal, relative to some target organization. A very dedicated attacker is going to spend a lot more than just a couple of hours looking for an opportunistic bug. For instance, a terrorist group may spend months if not years planning an attack against their target, and they will not stop in many cases until they figure out a way to accomplish their goal; same thing with a nation state.

Sample Adversary

Adversary	Threat profile										
	Commitment				Resources				Skills and capabilities		
	Intensity	Stealth	Time	Primary motivation	Personnel	Kinetic	Access	Technical	Physical security	Social engineering	Financial resources
Skilled remote attacker	H	H	Weeks	Financial	2 - 9	N/A	L	H	← N/A H		→ M

Attacker can outsource the same way a business can

Beyond that the financial resources I mentioned, an attacker with a large amount of financial resources can outsource their efforts in the same way that a business can. Basically if they want to get their hands on certain information or certain levels of access, they may go through and start blackmailing people or bribing employees to give up passwords or to willingly go click on a link that provides a shell to their hacking team. Or they can just go hire very skilled individuals to go carry out certain attacks and kind of modularize and compartmentalize their attacks on an organization.

Sample Adversary

Adversary	Commitment				Resources				Skills and capabilities		
	Intensity	Stealth	Time	Primary motivation	Personnel	Kinetic	Access	Technical	Physical security	Social engineering	Financial resources
Skilled remote attacker	H	H	Weeks	Financial	2 - 9	N/A	L	H	N/A	H	M

An insider will likely not require the same level of social engineering and physical security skills as an outside attacker will

The last one here is the level of access. For instance, with an insider threat, one humorous example jumps to mind, are the guys from Office Space. They were all employees so they had access to the system that they needed to write this money ciphering malware on and upload it appropriately. If a similar attacker from the outside was trying to do that, they would first have to get access to the internal network and go from there, and then learn about it and then write the malware then carry out the attack. An attacker with insider access already has their access badge. Employees already know them; they're not going to be suspicious just walking around a facility. They may not require the same level of skills that an outside attacker would, but in this case for the skilled remote attacker, they have low access, which means they don't have any access initially in our matrix, so therefore to do any kind of people-based skills or onsite physical security tests or anything like that they will need a much greater degree of social engineering skills and prowess to carry out those attacks.

Things to Keep in Mind

- Some variables can influence or directly impact others
- Not all adversaries are wholly concerned with "cyber" based attacks
  - Criminal organizations
  - Insider theft
  - Espionage
  - Terrorist unit
- Need to keep a consistent grading scale across all adversaries

A couple of things to keep in mind, I mentioned this first one—variables can influence either directly or indirectly other variables. You don't need an exact mapping of how everything fits together, but you just have to keep it in mind as you're writing up your report and carrying out your analysis.

The other thing is not all adversaries are going to be fully concerned about cyber-based attacks. Some adversaries, as we saw with the unfortunate events of 9/11, cyberattacks were not an issue although there were still a few different vulnerabilities leading up to that that allowed that attack to take place. You have to consider the motivations of your particular adversary with regard to what kinds of things they're going to carry out.

Bringing Software In

- Software is what's actually handling our sensitive assets (e.g., SQL queries, page content generation, session management, etc.)

- Portfolios can range from 1to10 up to several thousand

- Can be a mix of COTS or homegrown

- Scanning the network doesn't give you the complete picture, but neither does just focusing on the software

As many people reading this book know, software handles a lot of our sensitive data, from our banking information when we log in on our mobile devices, to the page content that comes up when we browse to some lending site or portfolio management site, to the session management that links our Gmail and Facebook accounts to all the other things that are using Single Sign On (SSO)-based functionality.

Application portfolios for a particular organization can range from just a handful to ten flagship apps, or one flagship app, and a couple of supporting services, up to several thousand in the case of large financial services organizations or government agencies. These application portfolios can be a mix of commercial off-the-shelf software, or they can be homegrown software, or they can be all of one or all of the other. Of course, scanning just the network does not give you the complete picture. But of course, just scanning the software does not give you the complete picture either and doing both does not give you the complete picture because then you're neglecting different processes and people, etc. Really this leads into why we need to make sure that we consider software in our testing methods because of its importance and relevance to the assets that we're targeting.

High Risk of Low Risk

- Shared assets across components:

  - Credentials, authentication portals, session cookies, frameworks, etc.

- Subdomains can be used to attack parent domains

- Cross-component customer support

We touched on this before with the high-risk or low-risk discussion, essentially flipping risk management on its side. And this is really where you run across different things that you're measuring and assigning risk to. You have shared assets or shared features, or shared functional components such as customer service roles, or single sign on cookies, or authentication portals or technical framework etc.

CHAPTER 7

Composite Attacks

Composite Attack Scenario

- Low-risk application that was never tested on a subdomain of a high-profile application

- Insecure session cookies

- Configuration flaws in network devices

- Missing 2FA on administrative VPN

- Internal apps could be accessed with legit session cookies to transfer $$$

In another composite attack involving a financial services company, we modelled a sophisticated criminal organization that was focused on accessing customer financial data. We found their flagship application had a lot of different security controls in place; everything was very well guarded. On a subdomain of that high-risk flagship application, we found a marketing site, let's call it marketing acmebank.com. It was just a promotional site. We found that subdomain was riddled with various injection issues, SQL injection, XSS issues, etc. We also noticed that the session cookies for both of those applications, because it was a subdomain, were scoped to the parent domain, well not because of, but they happened to be scoped to the parent domain and they were not protected with either the secure or HTTP only flags.

We also found a flaw on their mail server that allowed a local only open relay where we could send mail from any acmebank.com e-mail address that we chose such as admin@acmebank.com to any employee internal acmebank.com e-mail address. We therefore put together a phishing attack that redirected people to our cross-site scripting payload on that marketing acmebank.com web site. We created the attack to steal domain credentials, and at the same time we posted their cookies back to a server we controlled as is normally the case in many cross-site scripting payload scenarios or cross-site script exploitation scenarios. What we did was take those credentials and we found one particular VPN end point out of five that was missing two-factor authentication. We used those credentials to log in to the VPN end point and that gave us access to the internal network. From there, we did a little more scanning and moving around we found the application that was more of a customer support-focused application where customer support agents could transfer money from account to account. Interestingly that internal application was protected with two-factor authentication as well given its sensitivity within the organization; however, because we had phished several users of that role, we were able to use their cookies from our attack because this was also a subdomain of our original target application, we are able to use those cookies to bypass the two-factor authentication and get access to the application with their access rights and we found that we could transfer money to and from arbitrary accounts in that case. Again moving from absolutely nothing to a complete remote attack to achieve that goal. In this particular composite attack, leveraging social engineering, leveraging application layer attacks, leveraging network layer attacks, and the fact that a few bigger flaws around session management and cookies as well as low hanging fruit vulnerabilities, all weaved together.

Composite Attacks

- An end-to-end attack that leverages a string of weaknesses to compromise an objective

- This is a real-world attack scenario

- We can map these composite attacks out in a matrix and find specific vulnerabilities or process weaknesses that are leveraged in a variety of attacks

- Overlapping issues can help us highlight risk and prioritize remediation

Composite attacks as we mentioned are really the end attack scenarios that go from nothing to achieving a goal. When you're mapping these things out it can be helpful to map them out in a matrix-based format, and when you do this, you can identify different steps in a composite attack where similar types of vulnerabilities may be popping up in different composite attacks that you are trying out. In doing this it can help you as a consultant or as somebody trying to help somebody else defend a system, come up with better ways to prioritize remediation efforts against those issues that keep popping up. For instance, if there's one SQL injection or one buffer overflow that is used in five out of ten composite attacks, then you may want to make sure that that particular issue is fixed before anything else because it's critical to fight different composite attacks.

Attack <-> Defense

- Attack
  - Ongoing vulnerability scanning
  - Targeted penetration testing (technical and non technical)
  - Static system or code review

- Defense
  - Monitor (network and application appliances)
  - Detection (IDS, WAF, etc.)
  - React (IP blocking, account lockouts, etc.)
  - Logging

Moving into the bridging attack and defense efforts. So attack efforts are really anything regarding the vulnerability scanning, the pentesting, the code review, anything offensive, and anything that focuses on reviewing components from that bug discovery perspective. Defense is really all about identifying issues as they're coming in or identifying attack efforts, monitoring the state of things, and of course reacting to things and logging stuff. That way you have it for forensic purposes.

Bridging the Gap

- During a red team, log all "active" testing activities for log correlation

  - Analyze for discrepancies in detection capabilities

- Take notes on all places where attacks are blocked

- Keep all tool-generated logs and screenshots throughout the test

- Log aggregators can be used for automated cross-referencing given the correct formats and some customization

Bridging the gap between these things, during a red team you want to make sure that you log any and all testing activities that you have or that you generate during a test. We log all active testing activity, because passive activities such as reconnaissance do not involve interacting with employees or systems, and as such, we are not going to generate anything that would be logged by their systems. You don't have to log any of that, but keep a log of any and all active testing whether it's a manual spreadsheet based log, or whether you're taking a bunch of tools, tool-based output, and keeping screenshots. All of that is interesting to defenders and at the end of the engagement, or if you're doing more of an ongoing engagement model, you can aggregate it into log aggregating tools like Splunk, for instance, and you can use that to cross-reference certain things and identify potential gaps in a detection technology, or in a detection filter, and ultimately help that organization write better filters or log in additional places, or whatever the case is to better detect and subsequently react to attacks.

CHAPTER 8

Conclusion

Concluding Remarks

- Planning cannot be undervalued from both a business and technical context

- Clearly define goals and adversaries thant should be attacked and modeled, respectively

- The red team should test and rank risk from the adversaries' perspective

- Achieving a goal != finding a lot of vulnerabilities

Planning a red team is something that you can't brush off and just jump right into. You need to understand everything from a business and technical context before you get started. With that goes having clearly defined goals, clearly defined adversaries that you can attack and model, respectively. Of course, a red team should test and rank risk from the adversary's perspective. A nation state is going to find a basic cross-site scripting as "lightweight," i.e., probably not very interesting. If we can't do anything interesting with it then the impact is probably a lower risk issue to them. Whereas in the case of a pentest where you're measuring a particular web app, cross-site scripting in that particular context may be ranked high. It's really all about what can you do with the particular vulnerability that makes it interesting.

The last point that we think is the most important point is that everyone should walk away from this test with it having achieved a goal. Compromising an adversarial goal does not automatically equal finding a whole lot of vulnerabilities. Remember that it is the asset that is being compromised that makes headlines not the vulnerabilities being identified.

Printed in the United States
By Bookmasters